He is NOT Left Behind... He is with ME!

A handbook to encourage parents, while offering tips for raising children

BRENDA A. JENKINS
DR. LORETTA J. MARTIN

FOREWORD BY CARL R. BOYD

*Priority*ONE
publications
Detroit, MI USA

He is NOT Left Behind... He is with ME! 2nd Edition
Copyright © 2008 Brenda A. Jenkins and Dr. Loretta J. Martin

All rights reserved. No part of this publication may be reproduced, stored in a retrieval system, or transmitted in any form or by any means – electronic, mechanical, photocopy, recording, or any other – except for brief quotations in printed reviews, without the prior permission of the publisher.

*Priority*ONE Publications
P. O. Box 725 • Farmington, MI 48332
(800) 331-8841 Nationwide Toll Free
(313) 893-3359 Southeast Michigan
E-mail: info@p1pubs.com
URL: http://www.p1pubs.com

ISBN 13: 978-1-933972-06-0
ISBN 10:   1-933972-06-8

Edited by Patricia A. Hicks

Cover design by Bob Ivory, Jr.
Ivory Coast Communications

Printed in the United States of America

ENDORSEMENTS

The last 30 years have proven that the more we leave the responsibility for training our children up to others, the greater the chance we will find that we have placed our babies in the pawnshop of ignorance. As parents we must do whatever we can to redeem them before others, who do not have their best interest at heart, attempt to purchase them for mere pennies on the dollar. In their book, *He is NOT Left Behind... He is with Me!*, authors Brenda A. Jenkins and Dr. Loretta J. Martin challenge and inspire us to do what it takes to trade in our children's downward spiral for the upward climb of significant contribution.

Derek Blackmon
Detroit Parent Network

When Parents show up, children straighten up emotionally, socially, and academically. This book shares some practical advice and keen insights on parenting in the 21st Century.

Della A. Ezell
Founder/Executive Director
Parenting Unlimited, Inc

Where do you learn how to parent in America? This is an excellent book for parents who want to be informed and empowered.

Dr. Jawanza Kunjufu
Author, Developing Positive Images and
Discipline in Black Children

This book captures the essence of the importance of the link between home and school. Successful educators have to believe that "Parents see children as an extension of THEMSELVES" There is spiritual connection throughout the text that assures-- He or She will NEVER be left behind. This is recommended reading for all parents and educators.

Nora Martin Ph.D.
Professor, Emeritus
Eastern Michigan University

Table of Contents

Endorsements 3

Acknowledgements 7

Foreword... 11

Introduction.. 13

Chapter One: Be a Lighthouse! 17
    Brenda A. Jenkins

Chapter Two: Healthy Parents 27
    Dr. Loretta J. Martin

Chapter Three: Healthy Families 45
    Dr. Loretta J. Martin

Chapter Four: Powerful Communications.................... 69
    Brenda A. Jenkins

Conclusion 91

Recommended Reading.. 93

About the Authors.. 95

Other Books... 99

Acknowledgements

Brenda A. Jenkins

To my heavenly Father whose spirit resides in my most inner being, thank you.

From my inception in my mothers womb, I have loved and been connected to my mother and father, the late William and Florestine Springer. As I grew I learned from everyone, thank you. Each person taught me a lesson. I would like to pour out to others what I have learned.

To my Aunt Martha, thank you for serving as my second mom.

To both of my deceased grandmothers, whom I had the pleasure of having long pass the death of my parents and two siblings, thank you.

To my brothers and sisters (Thomas, Louise, Willie James, Ronald, Marcus and Virginia), thank you for your love.

Thanks to my middle school counselor, Mrs. Hood, who encouraged me to attend Cass Technical high school.

Thanks to my high school counselor, Ms. Pat, who encouraged me to stay at Cass Technical high school.

To my deceased, first husband, Eddie Battle Sr., thanks for our four beautiful children.

To the Writers Resources and Accountability for Publishing team thank you for the encouragement and monthly meetings.

To my cousin Loretta Martin, mentor, co-author, thank you. I love you.

To my niece, Angela Thomas, my pre-editor, executive director who handles my speaking engagements, book signings and provides insight from a teacher's perspective. Thank you.

Special thanks to my birthday club, who I can depend on for dinner six times a year. I love you.

Acknowledgements

Dr. Loretta J. Martin

To God, who has the blueprint for my life, and allows me to follow the script that He has prepared for me.

To my parents, Eddie and Carrie Hall, who have made their transition; they were the first teachers for my sister and I, and model parents for the original residents of the Ida B. Wells housing projects in Chicago, Illinois.

To my high school principal, Dr. Virginia F. Lewis who at the age of 98, inspired me again by writing a book- "Short Stories from a Long Career."

To my mentors Alyce R. Holden, Melvin Peyton Martin, and Agis Bray, Jr., who recognized my talents and encouraged me in my formative years.

To my pastor, Rev. Dr. Jeremiah A. Wright, Senior Pastor of Trinity United Church of Christ, who has provided me with a weekly dose of his wisdom beginning on Christmas morning in 1981.

To Dr. Jawanza Kunjufu who helped to solidify my African centered mindset on the subjects of the family and education in my early years of teaching.

To my cousin Brenda, who inspired me and pushed me into writing. She has guided me in a direction that I have needed to go for a long time.

To Carl R. Boyd, my friend, advice teacher and author, who has a plan for the solution to problems of the African American family and will share it soon with all who will listen.

To my children; Joy, Deedra, Kim, Michael, and Kevin who have each played a part by sharing their talents to make this book a reality.

To my personal editor and grand daughter Melody Davis, who has spent a great deal of her time, making sure that I make sense.

To my cheerleaders; Griffin Ed Banks, Della Ezell, the Wendell Phillips H.S. family, sorors and my church family; including the Newness of Life Ministry and the Hurston Hughes Writers Group at Trinity UCC.

Foreword

Brenda A. Jenkins and Loretta J. Martin have "put their fingers on" - and their hearts into - THE critical component, relative to improving our society. They have focused on empowering parents. Often, the perception of the language of empowerment is that those who use it seek to make sure that those who are responsible for their offspring must assume sovereign authority over them; must be respected as their controlling disciplinarians; and, must be regarded as "the last word" in all decision making. And, actually, this might make sense in a world where so many of us lament the state of weak parent-child relationships, and the absence of the "village concept" in some communities, as it pertains to raising children.

How blessed we are to have this offering which empowers by presenting statements, stories and strategies that are encouraging and practical for all who are determined to help their children rise to the pinnacle of their potential. As an educator (for 41 years) who has polled other educators (formally and casually) about what is needed to make schools better, I can report unequivocally, that the most frequent response relates to strengthening the home.

What these authors have "their fingers on" is not only the pulse of what educators need, but also, the pulse of a society searching for a dynamic response to the myriad anti-social messages and patterns of behavior that are currently capturing the hearts and minds of our youth.

Many of us can recite Proverbs 22: 6 from our Holy Bible: "Train up a child in the way he should go, and when he is old he shall not depart from it." Not many of us, however, know how to do the training. He Is Not Left Behind... does not criticize those who do not know for not knowing; but rather, "empowers" them with information and inspiration.

The "Master of the metaphor" (and the parable and the simile...) was of course, the Master Teacher, Jesus Christ. Isn't it well that we have with us, this day, two which follow His example to help us to grow by helping us to know, while causing us to laugh, to cry and to take positive steps in the right direction?

Allow me, please, to answer my own question in the way that all readers shall, upon completing this work: "Yes! It is well. It is well, indeed."

Carl R. Boyd
The Advice Teacher

Introduction

"There are two lasting bequests we can hope to give our children. One of these is roots; the other, wings."
Hodding Carter

Excuse me?
My child left behind? How can that be? He's with me!

There is no way that a child can be left behind unless perhaps he is living in a 3rd world country, his entire family is dead and he is homeless with little or no resources. It is by no means right, but it is reality, even in the 21st century.

On another note, how can a child be left behind in America if he is with his first and most influential teacher, you, the parent along with your posse to care for him? It has often been said that it takes a village to raise a child. In this case, the posse represents the village: parents, grandparents, siblings, relatives, neighbors, the church, social service agencies, baby sitters etc.

The educational system is secondary to the parents and the posse. As parents, we loan our children to the educational system for 6 hours a day for approximately 180 days in a school year or, to put it another way, 1080 hours a year. We as parents control the other 7680 hours that remain in each school year. It is what we do with those hours that determines whether the child is left behind or not. The best scenario however, is to tie the posse and the school together to help our children become the best that they can be. We are in a modern day war: fighting for the minds of our children.

Think of parenting in a pyramid concept: The bottom tier forms the solid foundation, the second tier prepares you for solid bonding, the third tier prepares you for leaving the nest, and the fourth tier represents your goal of producing a legacy of healthy offspring. This first series will discuss preparing the solid foundation by being a lighthouse for your child, keeping healthy (both parent and family) and developing powerful communication skills.

Introduction

In the beginning of parenthood, you bring to the table your hopes and dreams for the child that you have brought into this world. In the early years you struggle really hard to help your children with their development: teaching them everything from walking, and talking, to eating, potty training, following directions etc. They are totally dependent on you for their well being and safety. They also begin to imitate parents and others in the family.

Change is inevitable, and there is growth despite the change. The next generation in the family will duplicate your style, change it to fit their goal and history repeats itself. If your family is not functioning as well as it can, let the better parenting skills begin with you, then, no one in the family will be left behind.

~ CHAPTER ONE ~
Be a Lighthouse

Brenda A. Jenkins

"Do what you can, with what you have, where you are."
– Theodore "Teddy" Roosevelt

Sonja Carson had some obstacles rearing two sons in the southwest area of Detroit, Michigan. She was a single mom. One day one of her sons, Ben, came home with a bad report card. Sonja was overwhelmed. She prayed and then developed a plan. Even though she only had a 3rd grade education, she knew the value of reading. Sonja required her sons to read two books a week and complete a book report for each book. This was over and above their regular homework. They could not go outside to play or watch TV until their homework and book reading were done.[1]

---

[1] Carson, B., & Murphey, C. (1996). <u>Gifted Hands: The Ben Carson Story.</u> Grand Rapids, MI: Zondervan.

Both boys' grades improved as their knowledge base increased. Today, the oldest son is an attorney and the youngest, Ben, is the best pediatric neurosurgeon in the world. Sonja prayed, had a plan and was consistent with her plan. She knew the boys could check out books at the library for free and she was consistent with her discipline. Her story proves that if you do what you can, with what you have, right where you are then your children will be less likely to be left behind.

Many adults may feel our children are lost in the midst of our fast paced society today. We all can play a part by teaching our children what we have learned. In this chapter we will discuss how adults can do what they can, with what they have, right where they are in life. As adults, we can share our current skills with youth in our circle of influence. By doing so, we can become a lighthouse.

In the United States the first lighthouses were built to foster the growing economy of the colonies. Many preceded the birth of the nation. Think of our youth as our future leaders. Compare them with the birth of the nation or for easy reference birth of the future. Like the first lighthouse helped foster the growing economy, we can help foster our children's growth to become future leaders (lighthouses).

As we focus on what a lighthouse is and its purpose, let's consider ourselves a lighthouse, our child as the captain of their ship and the sea as society. Sonja Carson was a lighthouse in her sons' lives. Like her, with each skill we possess, we can illuminate the mind of a young person directly or indirectly. As adults, we provide the direction our youth need to navigate in today's fast paced society. Think about when you were a child. Who helped you learn to adapt to society? Look at our world today. Today they have technology (a society of its own) and much more interaction with the world's societies. All of our children are unique. Our skills are the light beams from the lighthouse. As children learn, they better navigate their ship at sea. The light from the lighthouse is powerful and is seen for miles by the ships at sea.

Likewise, our skills shared with our children can be a powerful source to help them succeed as they navigate their ships through multiple societies in the world today. Our forefather's journey is our civilization today. As we learn and share with our children, it will assist them in their journey for tomorrow's civilization. Our experiences, education (both formal and informal) and values determine who we are today. What kind of light are you projecting toward young people in your circle of influence? Let's provide our youth with many lights.

Parents and caregivers have home court advantage when it comes to rearing youth in their household. Typically, they know more about their child than others. Since parenting is not something most people are trained in prior to doing the job, we must do what we can, with what we have, where we are. The beauty of it all is that if we teach what we know (basic values and life skills) this will take our children a long way. These things can be taught as we model this behavior. Sonja Carson eventually learned to read, earned her GED and went to junior college. She was awarded an honorary doctorate.[2] Dr. Sonja Carson demonstrated how you can lead right now. Remember, do what you can, with what you have, right where you are in life.

Based on the 2004 US Census Educational Attainment Survey 83.9% of adults 25 and older attained high school diplomas and 27% of the adults 25 and older attained Bachelor's degree or higher.[3] From this same chart, individuals below poverty level attained 13.1% of high school diplomas. Data shows that educational attainment may impact economic level. Many of the statistics reflect measurable results from educational institutions. Now when it comes to statistics, some people may base major decisions on the data presented. My question is, what picture do these statistics paint? Who was included in the data? How many adults are in the circle of influence for each child? Do you have all the data you need to help assess how to help your child? As a lighthouse, we are guides. Let's discuss how we can provide direction to our youth.

Sometimes the news about what is happening with our youth is discouraging. Each of us has responsibilities to our youth. We must stay focused and be accountable for them. In our fast paced society, time is becoming a rare commodity. For our children time equals love.

---

[2] Fadiran, T. (2006, February 18) <u>Your True Hero</u>. http://www.yourtruehero.org/content/hero/view_hero.asp?2160

[3] U. S. Census Bureau. S1501 Educational Attainment. (2004) American Community Survey. http://factfinder.census.gov/servlet/STTable?_bm=y&-geo_id=01000US&-qr_name=ACS_2005_EST_G00_S1501&-ds_name=ACS_2005_EST_G00_

Our children are an investment in our future. As parents, we need to focus on rearing our children to be the best they can in what ever areas they are good in.

Dr. Thomas Armstrong's book, *You're Smarter Than You Think: A Kid's Guide to Multiple Intelligences*, discusses how our children are smarter than we think. Dr. Armstrong has followed Dr. Howard Gardner[4] who challenged the idea that IQ is the best measure of intelligence. Dr. Armstrong states, "Being smart isn't only about getting good grades, scoring well on test, and memorizing stuff."[5]

While I won't discuss the eight multiple intelligences here, I will encourage you as a parent or caregiver to recognize that you have many skills to share with your child. Use what you've got right where you are in life. If each adult taught one child, it may lessen the roughness of society from the child's perspective.

All of us have skills that we can share. What are some of your skills that you can share with a child? Cooking, sewing, balancing a checkbook, dancing, singing, reading, talking with people, problem solving, overcoming negativity, writing, speaking, and integrity are some examples of skills. Look at the picture of the child and the lighthouse. How can you provide the light (your skills) that the child in the picture needs?

---

[4] Armstrong, T., Ph.D. (2003) You're Smarter Than You Think: A Kid's Guide to Multiple Intelligences (Minneapolis, MN: Free Spirit Publishing, Inc). 2.

[5] Ibid, 1.

"The best way you can predict your future is to create it."
Stephen Covey

Another example of a parent doing what she could, with what she had, right where she was, is the mother of Ray Charles. She had a fourth grade education.[6] In the movie, *Ray* (the life story of Ray Charles), there were many lessons Ray learned from his mother. Ray's mother was navigating her ship through the obstacles of life and teaching him to be independent. His mother told him she would show him one time. If he made a mistake, she would help him. The third time he was on his own.

For those that have not seen the movie, think of a time when you were in a situation that you felt helpless only to discover that you already had all the skills you needed. Your self-confidence may have been low. After you were motivated by a bright light, your self-confidence improved. In the movie, the lessons Ray's mother taught

---

[6] Ray Charles Enterprises, Inc. (2006, February 18). http://www.raycharles.com/the_man_autobiography.html

him were independence and to use all of his senses. Ray's mother also told him not to let anyone make him a cripple. Near the end of the movie, when Ray was in rehabilitation for drug addiction, his memory of his deceased mother's words was clear. He recalled the light beam (lesson) that she taught. It was said that Ray never used drugs again.[7] If you review Ray Charles' autobiography, you will see he had other lighthouses as he grew up. Some examples were Mr. Pitman showing him how to play melody on the piano with one finger and Ma Beck who helped him through his depression after his mother's death.[8] Ray may be considered "Music Smart."[9]

Our role as parents lasts a lifetime. There are always lessons to teach and lessons to learn. Every one is different and learns differently. Let's say Ben was considered "Nature Smart" and Ray considered "Music Smart."[10] They both learned albeit differently and that was OK. Allow children as captains of their ship to learn from where they are from you. As we grow, our children grow. We are their primary role models.

As a parent, I had so many challenges rearing my children as a single working mom that I could write a book just on the challenges alone. I have four young adults. I asked each to name two skills they learned from me. They said independence, character, respect,

---

[7] Hackford, T. (Director). (2004). <u>Ray</u> [Film]. Hollywood: Universal Studios.
[8] Ibid.
[9] Armstrong, pg. 3.
[10] Ibid.

cleanliness, importance of education, and thinking. As someone who values effective communication, my preference is to share skills that are being used by some of the captains within my circle of influence. To provide the answers of my young adults is to share from their perspective what skills they learned. Communication is two way. The skills that were successfully learned are better told by them. As a light for those in my circle of influence, I share continuously.

What would those in your circle of influence say they have learned from you? It is my hope that the following exercises will give you the information you need to be the lighthouse you can be, where you are, with what you have right now, for the captains in your circle of influence.

EXERCISES:
1. List your skills. (Ability to explain yourself, self respect, loving others, etc.)
2. What skills are you sharing to help your child navigate their way? (Self respect, love, balancing a checkbook, etc.)
3. What ways are you sharing? Give examples. (I mentor adolescent girls, Girl or Boy Scout leader, youth director at recreation center, etc.)

4. What is your vision of your child's future as it relates to your child as an adult? (A child that is mentally, physically and spiritually fit)
5. Who were some of the lighthouses in your life? (Parents, school counselors, aunt or uncle, teacher, mentor)
6. What skills did the lighthouses assist you in developing? (Believing in myself, always do your best; don't compare yourself to others, etc.)
7. How did those skills help you? (Similar to number 6)

SUGGESTIONS:

1. Let your light beam shine.
2. Influence the child/young children in your life.
3. Get to know people (what are their desires, pains, fears).
4. Help by keeping yourself physically, mentally and spiritually healthy.
5. Truth is important. It may help as a time management tool. Do not waste time blaming or defending.

It started when I was born.
I was alone, scared and cold.
I depended on others to provide me with relationships,
security and warmth.
Being a child I watched.
As I grew I took on the characteristics I saw.
I learned quickly so I would survive.

Now I am alone, scared and cold.
I am in darkness,
Looking for a light,
To show me the way.
Can somebody help me?

B. Springer

~ CHAPTER TWO ~
Healthy Parents

Dr. Loretta J. Martin

Have you ever applied for a job that required no experience, no education and no training? On this job, you don't have to have an interview, present a resume, take a test or be on probation for 60-90 days. This position requires that you be a teacher, leader, helper, policeman, preacher, cheerleader, cook, cleaner and much more. You will be paid even if you don't do a good job. It is the most challenging job you'll ever have and the retirement benefits will determine your success. According to the Sinai Parenting Institute[1] this position is called *parenting*. They define parenting as:

> *The developing of a relationship where a father, mother, or significant others take on the responsibility of molding the life of a child on a daily basis. To place within a child the values, morals, and life principles that will take it from a life of total dependency to a life of independency.*

---

[1] Sinai Parenting Institute – Curriculum. (2005). Chicago, IL.

In other words, if we do a good job, we are eventually going to work ourselves out of a job.

I'M A PARENT ALREADY. WHY DO I NEED TO BE HEALTHY?

When adults are asked the question, "Who has been the most influential person in your life and why," most of the time, the answer will be – my parent(s). This means that if we as parents can be the best that we can be, by gathering all of the information that we can get from those who have had some level of success, it may help us to be better parents. On the other hand, we can also learn from the mistakes of others and make a conscience decision not to follow that path and repeat the same mistakes.

It is important that we look at ourselves carefully and honestly. Are we taking good care of ourselves physically, mentally, socially, emotionally and spiritually? Are we lifelong learners, gathering and evaluating information from friends, teachers, books, magazines, motivational speakers, schools, libraries, the internet, the media, and other community resources? Those are the factors that describe a Healthy Parent.

You as a parent are probably already doing a good job. You want your children to be successful and you may long for the day that they will be all grown up. But let us not forget to enjoy the journey. Before you know it, they will be all grown up and ready to pursue their own dreams.

As parents, we want to learn as much as we can now, so that we won't have to say, "I wish I had known that when my children were very young." This chapter is written to help parents understand why it is so important for us to grow faster than our children are growing. We will look at the generation that has shaped us into the people that we are today. We will look at the needs that are common to all human beings, no matter what culture they live in. We will look at our issues, especially the unresolved ones. Lastly, we will look at some suggestions that will help us to overcome any barriers that interfere with the awesome job of parenting. We are all in this together, and by going *Back Down Memory Lane* and *Looking at the Man in the Mirror,* we will help each other to understand *Where Do We Go From Here*? We can solve many problems on our own, but we can also look at some solutions that may help us all rise to the top.

I. WHAT DO WE KNOW FOR SURE?
    a. Becoming a parent changes you forever.
    b. We all have our own ideas of what parenting is all about.
    c. A great deal of "who you are" can be traced to your family of origin.

When parenthood becomes a reality for a man and a woman, a new identity is established. Some see a new baby as a blessing from God, others may see it as a burden, some see it as extending the family legacy and others may see it as an interruption of plans. Some will receive it with much joy; others may see it with pain. Some will be relieved; others will be embarrassed. The list is endless, but one thing that we know for sure is that "parenthood changes you forever,"[2] regardless of the circumstances.

Not only did we have the experience of being parented ourselves, we have been influenced by observing others who were parenting or being parented. We have seen parenting situations in the movies and we have read material about parenting. We have all fantasized about the way we would do things if and when we became parents. The reality is however, that becoming a parent brings about joy for most people coupled with anxiety. The underlying question is, "Will I get it right, or will I mess it up?" Unfortunately, you won't know whether you've done a good job for a very long time.

Your family of origin is comprised of the people that you actually lived with in your childhood. Usually, it means the mother, father and siblings. Oftentimes the family of origin includes: "live in" grandparents, aunts, uncles, cousins and sometimes the friend of a parent who has been given parental authority.

---

[2] Ibid.

BACK DOWN MEMORY LANE

What are your memories of your own childhood? Were you reared in a family that met your **Fundamental, Psychological and Self-actualization needs?**[3] Did your parents show love and respect for each other whether they were together, separated or divorced? Were most of your childhood memories happy or sad ones? Were you and your siblings treated equally or was there favoritism? Did you live with more than your share of sadness, fear, blame, shame, guilt and anger? Or did you feel happy, accepted, proud, nurtured, free and loved unconditionally?

Regardless of the love you might have had for your family, did you secretly wish that you had not been born into your family, and did that wish last for a long period of time? Did "the village," commonly known as your extended family, school, friends, neighbors, church and community agencies enhance the things that your parents were doing? Or did those in the village have to rescue you (actively or passively) from the negative practices of your parents?

Did you make a decision in childhood that you would parent your children quite differently than you were parented? The shocking truth is that we either approved or disapproved of the way we were reared by our parents

---

[3] Maslow, A. <u>Motivation and Personality.</u> (1987). HarperCollins Publishers.

and fortunately or unfortunately, we are in many ways very similar to our own parents. If we are satisfied that our parents did a decent job of rearing us (even though they made some mistakes), we are fortunate. But if we are angry, bitter and unforgiving for what our parents did or did not do to us as children, we must let those feelings go. Our parents could only give what they received. In many situations, they thought they were right because they didn't know any better or they didn't know anything different (this was the way they were raised).

Remember, the art of parenting is **generational**; habits, rituals and values are passed down from one generation to the next. If we go back down memory lane, we can sort out the correct from the incorrect lessons learned, recognize the dysfunctional patterns and break the cycle of our family's faulty parenting skills.

Finally, we must remember to never use our parent's faulty parenting skills as an excuse or as a crutch for our own shortcomings. Maya Angelou encourages us to realize that, "When we know better, we do better." There is a huge surplus of resources that are available to us in this information age to help us *know* better.

In a pyramid that has become known as Maslow's Hierarchy of Needs, Abraham Maslow in his book entitled, *Motivation and Personality,* shows us that there are various levels of human needs.

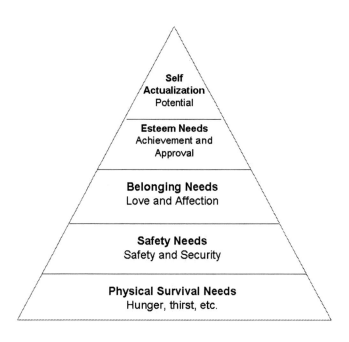

The most basic needs are at the bottom of the pyramid. If those are missing the human body can die (i.e. food and water). As we grow and mature, we become more complete and competent beings (as our needs higher on the pyramid are met). When there are unmet needs, we can end up with unresolved issues.

1. *Physiological Needs: to satisfy hunger, thirst, sex drive, and body nutrients.*
2. *Safety Needs: to feel secure, safe, and out of danger.*
3. *Belonging Needs: to feel loved, to affiliate with others, be accepted and to belong.*

4. Esteem Needs: To achieve, be competent, gain approval and recognition.
5. Self-Actualization: The need to fulfill one's unique potential.

This theory is respected by the great thinkers around the globe. One could hardly ever pick up a book on psychology and fail to find Maslow's Theory in it. Unfortunately, most high schools do not teach psychology or related subjects and the exposure is mostly available to those who seek higher education.

Some of us had no idea that Maslow's Theory could put a face on our basic needs that shows us about how our basic needs must be met before we can navigate our way up the pyramid to become our best self.

II. WHAT DO WE KNOW FOR SURE?
    a. Our unresolved issues are brought with us into the parenting experience.
    b. One of the worst things that can happen is for us to be unaware of our unresolved issues.

We all have issues. An issue can be described as a problem or a concern that needs to be discussed or resolved, so that it is no longer a problem or a concern. An issue could be a minor one such as, "What will I do to keep from gaining more weight?" Or it can be a major one such as, "How do I get out of this abusive relationship?" Issues usually don't go away unless you do something to make them go away. A good way to resolve an issue is to <u>think</u>, <u>plan</u> and <u>act</u>.[4] That is to say: think about what it is you want to do, plan how you will do it and then do it. Many issues are never resolved because most people think and plan, but never make the final step of acting on the issue. Issues that continue over time are labeled unresolved issues.

If nothing is done to eliminate the issue, it usually continues and escalates into a more critical situation. In the examples above, we can see that the minor issue of weight gain, if unresolved over time, could result in obesity and create major health problems. What was once a <u>minor</u> issue has now become a <u>major</u> one. The abusive relationship could have ended with a critical injury or even death if no action was taken. The major issue that was unresolved then turned into a tragedy.

It is virtually impossible for your children to be unaffected by your unresolved issues. Children are very intuitive and will sense your moods, your emotions, your anxieties and your fears. What are you modeling for your children – the ability to meet a challenge head on or to suffer in silence by doing nothing and just let things happen to you? Never forget that "our children are actors, and they act out what they see in us."[5]

---

[4] Duster, A. Graduation Speaker – Wendell Phillips High School. June 1980, Chicago, IL.
[5] Kunjufu, J., Dr. Speaker – Hall-Marks Family Reunion, August 1992, Chicago, IL.

Unfortunately, we are unaware of some of our unresolved issues. Too often, as children, some of us encountered emotional experiences, some of them traumatic, but we never received the help that was needed to process the facts. We were never relieved of the negative emotions that may have resulted in the experiences. We were never healed so that we could move on to a more peaceful existence. What possibly happened was the fact that maybe no one knew how desperately we needed counseling or some type of professional help to overcome the emotional or traumatic experience.

Some examples of unknown issues are: abandonment, abuse (physical, mental, social, emotional or spiritual), adoption, alcoholism or other drugs, death of a parent or close relative, divorce, a parent that is in prison, gender identity, personal injury or illness, rape or being a witness to violence. Bringing these unresolved issues, also called "baggage," into adulthood and parenthood can result in: making poor choices or unwise decisions, engaging in poor relationships or exhibiting strange and sometimes violent behavior.

III. WHAT DO WE KNOW FOR SURE?
    a. Your self-esteem is affected by a variety of experiences.
    b. Self-esteem develops over time.

Self-esteem is your self image or how you feel about yourself. You may have positive feelings or negative feelings about yourself. These feelings are based on the relationships with people at home, in school, in your social life, on the job and in society. Parents who feel good about themselves can and usually pass the same feelings on to their children. These parents send positive messages of self-esteem to their children by letting them know that they are lovable and capable. Parents who do not feel good about themselves will likely pass the same feelings to their children. These parents send negative messages of self-esteem to their children by letting them know that they are unlovable and not capable.[6]

Most of what we learn about ourselves begins with the family. The family provides our major source of learning about who we are. As we are exposed to others, we learn more about the way they see us as individuals. No single person or event can determine our level of self-esteem. It develops over time and it constantly changes as we go through life.

MAN IN THE MIRROR

"He who looks outside his own heart, dreams, he who looks inside his own heart, awakens."   Carl Jung

We all have private thoughts about ourselves. There are secrets inside each of us that we may have never shared with anyone. But if we are truly honest with ourselves, we can make our own assessment by going back to the time when horrific events occurred in our lives. Once we

---

[6] Sinai Parenting Institute – Curriculum. (2005). Chicago, IL.

realize that they were not our fault, it becomes clear to us that we were victims and not bad little girls or boys. Most of us cannot make a self-assessment but need to get the help of a friend or professional. Whatever the method of discovery, a breakthrough of our past hurts including the pain, shame, guilt and other feelings will open our eyes to the truth so that true healing can begin. We cannot afford to live in denial of the hand that life has dealt us. We must accept ourselves as we are and make the most of our God-given talents. If we fail to do that, we are doing a disservice to ourselves and ultimately to our children.

Singer and entertainer, Mary J. Blige, had a breakthrough when she realized that her self-esteem was very low because of her past. The molestation that happened to her at the age of five, coupled with her mother's issues, was at the root of her pain and shame.[7] It was not until she prayed to God and received help from a man who eventually became her husband, that she understood herself. She declared that "there is a lot of pain when you learn that you're ignorant." The successful singing career, the money, the alcohol, THE drugs and the people around her did not bring her true happiness.

For years she blamed her mother and everyone else for her unhappiness. It was not until she looked in the mirror to find out who she really was, that she realized she was not living the life that God intended for her. Friends were

---

[7] Blige, M.J. (2006, February 1). The Oprah Show. ABC-TV.

dying, and like her, living the lifestyle of drinking, partying and the "bling." No one seemed to be telling the young entertainers the truth about life. Mary's incredible breakthrough came as she forgave the molester as well as her mother who had issues of abuse. Mary now understands her mother, stating: "I blame her for nothing, I forgive her for everything."

When you ask the question, "Who am I," make sure that you deal with your feelings. Ask yourself some realistic questions and answer them honestly: Who am I really?

1. The best thing about being me is…
2. The worst thing about being me is…
3. I see myself as…
4. If I could change anything about myself, I would change…
5. More than anything else, I would like to…
6. I have the power to…

WHERE DO WE GO FROM HERE?

"Change your attitude and gain your altitude."
Donald Trump

When you change, you may lose some friends. But then, were they really your friends after all or were they merely your associates? True friends will accept you as you are, no matter how much you change, for better or worse.

One of the best habits that we can have is to look at winners. Winners do things that others are unwilling to do. They go the extra mile to get things done. They don't make excuses, they make arrangements. Who are your role models? Are they admired by many people? Do they get respect from adults and children? Do they make the world a better place? Are they truly happy or are they simply putting on a happy face?

We know that looking at our own family of origin can help us to understand why we are the way we are as adults. We know that our families, no doubt, wanted the best for us and we want the same for our children. We also have looked at the fact that many of our behaviors are passed down from one generation to the next whether those behaviors are positive or negative. We have taken a look at the awesome job of parenting. It is a complex job that requires many skills that we already have, but we know that there is always room for improvement.

Thank God that we are receptive and open to new ideas. Otherwise, we would be stuck in a cycle of having the same problems, generation after generation. We are survivors and we understand now, more than ever, how important it is to work on ourselves. We are our children's first teacher and role model. If we want our children to have an even better life than we have, we must give them all the advantages and resources that are available today and we must seek the help of others to do so.

SOME SUGGESTIONS FOR SOLUTIONS
To Create a Healthy Mind, Body and Soul [8]

<u>LIFE IS A JOURNEY</u> – In every experience, there are <u>LESSONS LEARNED.</u>

1. Develop a personal philosophy of life and then live it.
2. Use a problem solving technique such as: What is the problem? What caused it? What is the solution? How do we solve it?
3. Make a plan and stick to it: some short term, others long term.
4. Get organized, keep a calendar and a "to do" list.
5. Protect your assets. Your name is the first asset.
6. Listen and learn from the elders, know your heritage.
7. Develop a family creed or code of conduct to live by.
8. Take responsibility for the education of your children, both in and out of school. Almost everything has a "teachable moment" element in it.

<u>DAILY MANAGEMENT</u> – Health is important. <u>LET THERE BE PEACE.</u>

1. Take good care of yourself and those for whom you are responsible.

---

[8] Martin, L. (2005, November 18). <u>13th Annual Youth Guidance Retreat.</u> Itasca, IL.

2. Work on your self-esteem, this determines many of your choices.
3. Identify your passion and make it work for you.
4. Expand your knowledge, learning is lifelong: read, go to school, seminars, plays, lectures, tapes, positive talk shows (radio & TV), volunteer and travel.
5. Keep a journal and write in it every day. This is free therapy for you.
6. Share your knowledge with others and learn from them too.
7. Pamper yourself and allow others to pamper you. After all, you deserve it.

PROTECT YOURSELF – You are your own best friend and DON'T APOLOGIZE FOR IT.

1. Learn to say NO and mean it! Then reward yourself by feeding your soul.
2. Get out of that rut. Doing the same things and expecting different results is a sign of insanity.
3. Protect your feelings, say: "When you…, it makes me feel…, and I don't like feeling that way. In the future, I would appreciate it if you wouldn't…"
4. Don't let them play games with you, say, "Are you trying to make me feel (choose one) guilty, stupid, ashamed, like a loser, etc? Remember, no one can deny to you your feelings. Those are your feelings and not theirs.

5. When faced with a tough decision, ask yourself, "What would _____ do?" (someone that you hold in the highest regard: a parent, mentor, hero, etc.)

6. When an adult asks a question that is too bold, say, "Why on earth would you ask such a personal question?" Watch them squirm, back off, apologize or deny it. If they don't do any of these, "LOVE THEM FROM A DISTANCE."

THE BALL IS IN YOUR COURT PARENTS. NOW RUN WITH IT!

Our society will be so much better when we have Healthy Parents who will in turn, provide us with Healthy Families. When our families are healthy, it will be very difficult for our children to be left behind.

~ Chapter THREE ~
Healthy Families

Dr. Loretta J. Martin

ARE YOUR CHILDREN DODGING BULLETS OR CHASING OPPORTUNITIES?

Could there ever be a higher calling in life than to have the privilege of loving and caring for children that you brought into the world? What could be better than to have children who revere God and serve others for a lifetime? Parenting is so much more challenging today. Our children are bombarded with topics that rob them of their innocence at an early age such as alcohol, drugs, sex, deviant behavior and rebellion. What's a parent to do? Peers often have more influence than the parents, schools and churches. Beside these concerns, many of our children are dodging bullets instead of chasing opportunities to be self-actualized with those at the top of the pyramid.

Even in households with two parents, raising children is an enormous task. We can be our own worst enemy if we try to be super parents with a lone ranger mentality. Not only do we need our extended families, both near and far, but we must broaden our resources or we will burn out and then be useful to no one.

In this chapter we will take a look at some things that just might work for you as you prepare to do what it takes to make sure that your child has the best opportunity to be the best that he/she can be. We will look at how you can tap into the village to accomplish some of your goals. We will look at the three systems that families operate out of and evaluate what we can do with that information. We will look at parenting styles and see how we can maintain control without giving up our power as parents. We will then look at one person's philosophy that has been adopted by many of us. This philosophy involves putting God first, your health second, your family third and then helping others to live a better life with some intervention. Once you develop a philosophy, whether it is this one or another one, you will at least have a philosophy and if you live by it, everyone will know exactly where you stand and they will respect you for taking that stand, whether they agree with you or not.

EVERY PARENT NEEDS TO KNOW
Families all operate under one of three systems: open, closed and healthy. Let's look at these more closely.

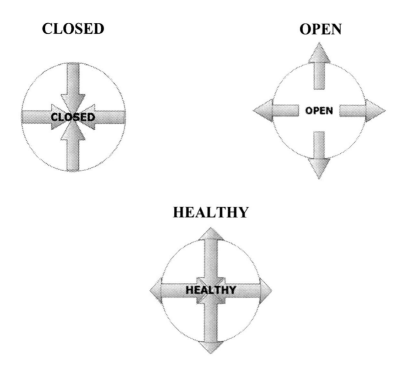

In a closed system, the family is very close. This seems admirable, but when the family is too close this is not good. The children are not allowed to participate in outside activities unless the parent is right there to watch every move. These children are smothered. The parents make all of the decisions, answer the phone, answer the door, etc. This family refuses counseling unless forced to get it. They don't believe in airing their dirty laundry. This family also has a lot of family secrets. The children's "gang" is at home, not in the streets.

The open family system is at the opposite extreme. This seems admirable but when the family is too open, this is not good. The children are given too much freedom. They hardly see their parents. Since their parents are "busy" they leave notes for each other. And there is not a lot of structure. Parents will buy a lot of gifts because they feel guilty for not spending time with their children. They will allow counseling, as long as they don't have to participate because their schedule is too hectic. When parents are very busy, all kinds of things could be happening in the basement such as hiding a runaway, selling drugs, etc. Friends come and go freely and make themselves at home there. It is easy for children in this type of household to be recruited into a gang.

The healthy family operates somewhere in the middle of these two extremes. They have family time together, but everyone gets to be alone sometimes. This family can be close, but not so close that they feel smothered. There is love, trust and a lot of other warm and fuzzy feelings that occur. But the children are disciplined when there is a need and a consequence when they screw things up. Life is not perfect but there is a lot of happiness here. These children are too busy to join a gang. Their needs are being met at home and through extra curricular activities.

Thoughts to Ponder

1. What was your family system as a child?
2. What is your family system now?
3. Do you know of families that are too closed?
4. Do you know of families that too open?
5. Do you know any healthy families?
6. Are you willing to change if your system is extreme?

WHAT IS YOUR PARENTING STYLE?

You will see parenting styles described by many sources of information. The description that I like best is the one by the Sinai Parenting Institute.[1] They are called Autocratic, Permissive and Democratic. As in the family systems, we have two extremes and one normal style.

Scenario
Dad says, "For our vacation this year, we're going to Cleveland, I haven't seen my brother in 5 years and he hasn't been well lately."

Autocratic Style
Son - "But dad, it's boring in Cleveland. I think we should go to Disneyland. It would be so much more fun."
Dad - "I said we're going to Cleveland and that's final."

---

[1] Sinai Parenting Institute – Curriculum. (2005). Chicago, IL.

Permissive Style
Son - "Oh that's boring! I'm going to Disneyland."
Dad - "Well, we'll see you later son, I've got to see my brother."

Democratic Style
Son – "But dad, it's boring in Cleveland. I think we should go to Disneyland."
Dad – "I tell you what son, if something happens to my brother, we will all regret not going. We'll all go to Cleveland this year and start saving money for Disney-Land next year."

As you can see, the autocratic parent says, "I'm the boss and what I say, goes." The permissive parent allows himself to be manipulated by the child. The democratic parent has his way, but allows for compromise.

A good way to let your children think they are making choices is by giving them two good choices such as, "Do you want an apple or an orange?"

ORGANIZE YOUR PRIORITIES
a. Getting our priorities straight is a big deal.
b. If we don't get our priorities straight, there are unhealthy consequences.

We seek to become better people, especially when we become parents. Sacrifices should and must be made because being a parent is a full-time job. No longer are we only responsible for ourselves. We must look out for the well being of others. No longer are we seen as an individual, we are now a family.

As one who is mentor to thousands, Dr. Jawanza Kunjufu states that we should keep our priorities straight. "Put God first, our health second, our family third, and then the liberation of our people."[2] That is a tall order for some, but it becomes easier when we begin to live with and practice such a philosophy every day.

WAKE UP!
PUT "GOD FIRST" IN EVERYTHING YOU DO

The apostle Paul wrote to Christians who had been trying to live in their own strength.

> *Are you so foolish? Having begun in the Spirit, are you now being made perfect by the flesh? Have you suffered so many things in vain if indeed it was vain? Therefore He who supplies the Spirit to you and works miracles among you, does He do it by the works of the law or by the hearing of the faith? Galatians 3:3-5 NKJV*

---

[2] Kunjufu, J., Dr. (2000). <u>Satan, I'm Taking Back My Health!</u> African American Images. Chicago, IL.

In other words the spiritual resources of character that Paul was talking about are not the result of trying to live by the ideals of God. They come when we believe and trust what God says He is willing and able to do in us.[3] Are you having problems with marriage, children, finances, relationships, etc.?

WAKE UP! It's all about putting God first in everything we do. We all have issues and we are all at different levels in our spiritual walk. Don't get nervous as we look (honestly) at our spiritual growth:

1. Do we spend time with God every day, or only once a week?
2. Do our actions speak louder than words? How do others see us?
3. Do we love as God loves?
4. Are we following in His Word?

The earlier that we realize that it's "All About God," the better our lives will be. The following poem was recited but never forgotten by a pre-teen. It sends a powerful message to all and causes us to think.

---

[3] RBC Ministries (2003) How Can a Parent Find Peace of Mind. Discovery House Books, Grand Rapids, MI

If Jesus came to your house

If Jesus came to your house to spend a day or two,
If He came unexpectedly, I wonder what you'd do.
Oh, I know you'd give your nicest room
to such an honored Guest,
And all the food you'd serve to Him
would be the very best,
And you would keep assuring Him
you're glad to have Him there,
That serving Him in your own home
is joy beyond compare.

But, when you saw Him coming,
would you meet Him at the door
With arms outstretched in welcome
to your heavenly Visitor?
Or would you have to change your clothes
before you let Him in?
Or hide some magazines
and put the Bible where they'd been?
Would you turn off the radio
and hope He hadn't heard?
And wish you hadn't uttered
that last, loud, hasty word?

Would you hide your worldly music
and put some hymn books out?

Could you let Jesus walk right in,
or would you rush about?
And I wonder, if the Savior
spent a day or two with you,
Would you go right on doing
the things you always do?
Would you go right on saying
the things you always say?
Would life for you continue
as it does from day to day?

Would your family conversation
keep up its usual pace?
And would you find it hard
each meal to say a table grace?
Would you sing songs you always sing,
and read the books you read,
And let Him know the things
on which your mind and spirit feed?
Would you take Jesus with you
everywhere you'd planned to go?
Or would you, maybe, change your plans
for just a day or so?

Would you be glad to have Him meet
your very closest friends?
Or would you hope they'd stay away
until His visit ends?

Would you be glad to have Him
stay forever on and on?
Or would you sigh with great relief
when He at last was gone?
It might be interesting to know
the things that you would do
If Jesus Christ in person came
to spend time with you.

Written by Lois Blanchard Eades[4]

Recited by Loretta Hall,
Olivet Baptist Church,
Chicago, IL. Early 1950's

---

[4] R. H. Boll, ed. <u>Word and Work.</u> (Vol. 49, No. 11, November 1955). Louisville, Kentucky.

WAKE UP!
YOUR HEALTH IS SECOND TO GOD

Our Physical Needs
All of the fame, fortune, beauty, education or success will mean nothing if you are not healthy. The quality of life changes drastically when the body breaks down. If we are in poor health, we cannot help ourselves or anyone else. We know that alcohol abuse destroys the family as well as the body, but what is killing us the most?

The major risk factors that lead to poor health are:

1. Tobacco use
2. Poor diet (coupled with a lack of exercise)
3. Obesity

Are you surprised at the above list? Let's explore these risk factors a little more. When we know better…

1. Statistics suggest that more people suffer from <u>tobacco</u> related diseases than from any other factors. The most common ones are: six types of cancer, heart disease, lung diseases (including chronic bronchitis and emphysema), ulcers, and circulatory diseases (stroke), etc. Smoking causes 90% of lung cancer deaths in men and 80% in women.

2. <u>A poor diet</u> consists of too much red meat, high saturated-fat, (animal) dairy foods like cheese and whole milk, and heavily salted, smoked and cured products like bacon and salami.

3. "There is an <u>obesity</u> epidemic in this country and treatment has focused on diet and exercise with relatively little success." Studies found that adolescents from close knit neighborhoods were less likely to be obese because of the collective efforts of neighbors who are willing to help each other, and many adults are role models for adolescents.[5] People who are obese are likely to suffer from the leading causes of death which are: heart disease, cancer, stroke, (and for African Americans) diabetes. These diseases are preventable with a proper diet and exercise. Unfortunately, there is often inadequate screening, late diagnosis and less aggressive treatment in far too many cases, especially for the poor.

What do people eat who have a low risk of the deadly diseases?[6]

1. If you are not a vegetarian, become a semi-vegetarian. Read and study about the various types of vegetarians.

2. Eat plenty of salads, greens, broccoli, carrots, tomatoes, onions and garlic.

3. Eat plenty of fruits, oranges, red grapes, strawberries, raspberries, blackberries, watermelons, etc.

---

[5] Cohen, D. Rand Health Study http://rand.org/news/press.06/02.09.html
[6] Women's Health. MSN Health and Fitness. February 06.

4. Eat dried beans, heavy and grainy bread, cereal bran and all kinds of nuts.
5. Drink plenty of water, green tea, and if you use milk, choose low fat.
6. Choose olive oil, canola oil or flaxseed oil instead of the traditional oils.
7. Choose oily fish, eel, turkey without the skin and some seafood.

More healthy hints[7]

- Breakfast is the most important meal of the day.
- Establish healthy eating habits and provide healthy snacks.
- Maintain a healthy weight.
- Exercise regularly at least 3 times a week for 30 minutes each.
- Develop a mind set of prevention that includes health and safety.
- Include hygiene in your prevention practices.
- Develop healthy sleep habits early in life.
- If you drink alcohol, drink moderately.
- You and your children must see your doctor(s) and dentist(s) regularly.

---

[7] Years Ahead. Helping Parents Grow Healthy Kids. http://www.yearsahead.com/Health_Tools/HealthBasics/HealthBasics.aspx/HB/GN01

- Seek new information on the internet, in books, magazines and newspapers.
- Limit your intake of sweets (cakes, candies, etc.) salty snacks (chips etc.), butter, margarine, cream, deep fried foods, egg yolks and organ foods such as liver.
- Learn to read labels and become a smart shopper.

But most of all let us share the knowledge. When we work together, we can all succeed.

We continue to be our children's role model and first teacher, which means that like us, they will not only grow spiritually with us, but they will take on our health habits as well. How wonderful it would be if we could begin serving healthy meals to our children from birth. No matter what age, we can begin wherever they are. We need to break old habits and develop new ones. We really have no choice when it comes to maintaining good health habits if we and our children are to be free of the physical ailments that plague our society today. What an awesome responsibility for parents, but we can and must do it.

WAKE UP!
YOUR FAMILY IS YOUR THIRD PRIORITY

WHAT DO WE KNOW FOR SURE?
a. It is virtually impossible to be happy if one's basic needs are not met.
b. If the family does not meet your basic needs, in many instances, you will seek them elsewhere.

In the Healthy Parent chapter, we looked at Maslow's Hierarchy of Needs Theory which is highly regarded by many experts in the field of Psychiatry. Earlier in this chapter we took a closer look at the two physiological needs that if not met, would prove to be fatal – the need for food and water. We took it to a higher level by looking at the quality of food and liquids that would assist in keeping our bodies healthy and at peak performance.

Now, we will look at the next level of needs as it relates to our families so that we operate at peak performance, commonly known as a healthy family. When the needs for safety, belonging and self-esteem are met, you then have the opportunity to reach the self-actualization need that is only met by a small fraction of the population. This level is one of extreme satisfaction and happiness and is "as good as it gets" in life.

SAFETY NEEDS [8]

a. *Control your children.* Every child needs to know there are limits to what he is permitted to do and that his parents will hold him to those limits; he must be taught self-control to avoid hurting himself and others when he feels jealous or angry.

b. *Guide your children.* Every child needs to have friendly help in learning how to behave towards persons and things; grown-ups around him show by example how to get along with others.

c. *Protect your children.* Every child needs to know that his parents want him safe from harm and that they will help him when he faces a strange or frightening situation.

d. *Provide a safe haven for your children.* Every child needs to know that his home is a place of safety, in which his parents will be at hand in time of need and that he belongs to and is an important member of the family.

e. *Create a Safe Environment for your children.* Every child needs to learn from his parents the rules and dangers of: alcohol and drugs, bike safety, sports safety, car safety, and the safety and danger of sex and sexuality.

---

[8] National Mental Health Association. What Every Child Needs for Good Mental Health. (February 2006) http://www.nmha.org/infoctr/factsheets/72.cfm

BELONGING NEEDS [8]

a. *Acceptance*
Every child needs to believe that his parents like him for himself, that they like him all the time and not only when he acts according to their ideas of the way a child should act; that they always accept him, though they may not always approve of the things he does.

b. *Faith*
Every child needs a set of moral standards to live by, a belief in human values such as, kindness, courage, honesty, generosity and justice.

c. *Love*
Every child needs to know that his parents love him, want him and enjoy him, that he matters to someone and that there are people around him who care what happens to him.

d. *Emotional Needs*
Every child needs to develop skills that will bring out the best in him; these skills include social skills, independence, responsibility and a sense of humor. [9]

---

[9] Channing-Bete Company. (2006). About Parenting. – http://www.channing-Bete.com

ESTEEM NEEDS

a. *Independence*

Every child needs to know that his parents have confidence in him and will help develop his ability to do good things for himself and others.

b. *Praise*

Every child needs approval and children, like adults, need a pat on the back for something good they have accomplished. This is not a small thing. It is important to the child.

c. *Recognition*

Every child needs to be recognized for what he is both inside and outside the home, so consider him in planning a new home, buying furniture, a new car or going on vacation.

d. *Success in School*

Every child needs to have success in school. Parents must be active participants in the education of their child. Schools should provide opportunities for students to receive recognition for attendance, scholarship, sports, academic events, etc. Parents must read to their child, encourage creativity and assist with homework. Turn off the T.V. Provide a place for homework and studying. Place a high value on education. Join parent organizations at school and talk with the child everyday about school. If unable to volunteer at the school, volunteer for a field trip.

Find out about you child's learning style and utilize it throughout his schooling. Provide books at home and insist that your child reads every day.

FOOD FOR THOUGHT:

We Learn and Retain:
- 10% of what we hear
- 15% of what we see
- 20% of what we both see and hear
- 40% of what we discuss with others
- 80% of what we experience or practice and…
- 90% of what we attempt to teach to other people

Therefore, make sure that your child tutors another child; even in subjects he is weak in. Results? Both of them reap the benefits. Or have them teach you what they are learning. It works wonders when they have to explain concepts.

IT REALLY DOES TAKE A VILLAGE TO RAISE A CHILD

We are all in this parenting thing together. Our community plays a big role in our well being. Studies have shown that children who grow up in neighborhoods that have good role models fare better in many ways.

Collectively we can do great things if we live and let live, love our neighbors, help each other and look out for the children in our neighborhood as well as our own. Have you ever heard of the crabs in a barrel mentality? Crabs pull each other down, so fearful that one will be better off than the rest. The end result? They all die together in the bottom of the barrel. If they were not so selfish, all of them would survive simply by allowing one crab at a time to climb out of the barrel.

In the housing project where I grew up, some people had crabs in a barrel mentality. It was customary for a jealous tenant to run and tell the housing administrators when a child matured and started working. The end result would be that the rent would be raised so high that the family couldn't afford to live there any longer.

I was blessed when my mentor (who took me under her wing when I was six years old) became the first African American woman to become a Chicago Park District supervisor. She hired me as a recreation leader at the age of 19. This meant that I could attend a private college to pursue my dream of becoming a physical education teacher like she had been. The public city college rejected 98% of the African American applicants who wanted to enter the program. It was my mentor who said, well go to another school. Isn't God awesome?

Even though my entire salary went toward my college tuition, books and transportation, my parents decided that we should move because we might be in trouble if we stayed there. My dad was a father figure to most of my friends and neighbors' children, therefore, there was a big void left when we moved because of a rule that didn't make sense to me and jealous people that didn't want to see anyone get ahead. This scenario was repeated over and over until most of the tenants who were upwardly mobile and good role models for others were gone. Those who remained in the community saw the community die a slow death, like the crabs in a barrel.

If you happen to live in a neighborhood that does not have a number of good role models, you will have to work hard to seek out the good people that will assist you with finding other positive people and experiences. You may be surprised to find that they are closer than you think, perhaps in the school, library, church, community centers, etc.

Keep your children busy. Remember the old adage – an idle mind is the devil's workshop. We can pull together collectively. We can help each other with the awesome task of raising our children and all rise to the top. The village is still alive and well. We are free to make sure that no children within our area of influence are left behind.

THE LIBERATION OF OUR PEOPLE

Liberation is a movement where one seeks equal rights and status for a group.[10] Everyone is in various states of

---

[10] Merriam-Webster Dictionary Online. http://www.m-w.com/dictionary/liberation. Main Entry: **lib·er·a·tion** Pronunciation: "li-b&-'rA-sh&n Function: *noun* **1** : the act of liberating : the state of being liberated **2** : a movement seeking equal rights and status for a group <women's *liberation*>- **lib·er·a·tion·ist** /-sh(&-)nist/ *noun*

bondage. When we, as parents, can liberate ourselves from our personal areas of bondage, then we will be able to help our children or those who we mentor out of their areas of bondage. Remember, no one is free until all of us are free.

As parents who really want a better world for their children, we must be willing to evaluate where we currently are so that we can set realistic goals in our efforts to ensure that our children are not being left behind. To evaluate your present condition answer the following questions.

SELF EVALUATION

1. Are you meeting the needs of your children?
2. Where is there room for improvement?
3. Do your eyes light up when your children enter the room?
4. Do you tell your children that you love them?
5. Do you hug them every day?
6. Do you give children what they need the most – your time?
7. What are you doing for the good of your race?
8. How do you liberate people who think they are free?

9. Will you accept the challenge to take the necessary steps to become more active in your child's development?

10. Write 5 things that you personally will to do to make this world a better place by liberating yourself and being an example of positive change.

1.

2.

3.

4.

5.

~ Chapter FOUR ~
Powerful Communications

Brenda A. Jenkins

"The way we communicate with others and with ourselves ultimately determines the quality of our lives."
Anthony Robbins

To communicate powerfully is to ensure your message is received by the intended person with the same meaning that you intended. When this happens, you become a powerful communicator. Communication is the exchange of information. Barriers that may interfere with the delivery of your message are: poor delivery, misunderstanding by the person(s) receiving the message, missing key information, emotions, differences, and wrong timing to name a few. When communicating your message, make sure the timing is right. You could be right but late. Your presentation may be the best but late. This chapter will discuss ways to make you communication powerful by using three principles:

1. Acquire Knowledge
2. Manage Emotions
3. Act with Purpose

Does anybody hear me? Have you ever asked yourself that question? Has what you said meant something different to the other person? Based on other's reactions or even having someone repeat what you said later in the conversation may be evidence that you were not understood. Do you feel betrayed? Could it be they really did not hear you? If your answer is yes to just one of these questions, it may mean there is room for more effective communication skills. Effective communication skills can benefit our communication with our kids, teachers and other people.

Dr. Harriet Lerner is a respected relationship expert. Dr. Lerner is a scholar on the psychology of women and family relationships. One of her books is *The Dance of Connections.* She defines what it means to have an "authentic voice" – one that runs counter to the automatic ways we try to speak our truths. It is vital that we learn to connect with people. Dr. Lerner says that having an authentic voice is not about speaking from anger but about speaking from core values and keeping our own immaturity in check.[1] She also discusses using wisdom and intuition as you decide what to say.

Acquiring Knowledge

According to Merriam-Webster's dictionary, knowledge is "the range of one's information or understanding." Another definition is "the branch of learning." When communicating a message it is important to know as

---

[1] Lerner, H. (2001). The Dance of Connections. HarperCollins Publishers, Inc. New York: New York

much as you can about yourself and the person(s) you are communicating with in order to help develop messages that are powerful. Acquiring knowledge of self may include being in touch with your desires, fears, pain, etc. Understanding and working through your feelings will be beneficial in order to communicate with power. When possible, attempt to learn as much as you can about the person(s) to whom you want to deliver the message. It may not always be possible. One way to do this is to listen to people with more than your ears. Also watch their reactions to messages and watch their actions. Gather and analyze this information as you create your message. Let's look at examples of how to communicate with purpose. This scenario is related to parenting. The incident is a fight at school.

SCENARIO

Lynn is a single working mom. Her work hours vary during the day. Her daughters, Lisa and Brandy, are in high school. Lynn receives a call at work from her daughter Brandy. She is very upset and crying. Brandy tells her mom another student jumped her from behind in the school lunchroom. She states that her sister tried to break up the fight. That is when the other student's sister jumped in along with one of their friends. Then Brandy states that her friend jumped in. Since it happened in the school lunchroom, they were all excluded for two weeks. Brandy is in the 9th grade and is an honor student. Lynn got off work and went home. Brandy was still crying. She states she is fearful that this incident will happen again. The student who jumped Brandy from behind is also an honor student.

A couple of months earlier they had a confrontation in one of their classes. Lynn has spoken with Brandy's teacher on two different occasions about her concerns with the two girls. For the last month everything had been quiet. Brandy said she did not know what the consequences of the fight would have on her position in the honor society. She is also concerned because she felt she had to defend herself. Brandy states, "It is not fair." Lynn and Brandy want to change schools now. Brandy cried herself to sleep.

Lisa, an 11th grader, is not crying. For Lisa this is just another day in school and she was not going to let anyone beat up her baby sister. What do we know? See Chart #1.

What We Know – Chart #1

Knowledge	Emotions	Does this have anything to do with what you want to communicate at this time?	Act with Purpose
Lynn – lost time (money) having to leave work early.			
Lynn – Her daughters are not safe – fight at school.			
Lynn – She has spoken to Brandy's teacher twice in the last 3 months.			
Lisa – jumped into the fight to protect her sister.			
Lisa – acts as if this is just another day at school.			
Brandy – is crying.			
Brandy – is worried about the impact this incident will have on her status in honor society.			
Brandy – wants to change schools.			
Brandy – feels she had to defend herself and it is not fair she is being excluded.			

How many issues can you identify with the information from this scenario? Which one would you deal with first? Lynn chooses to comfort her daughters.

WHAT COLOR ARE YOUR EMOTIONS?

Looking at the information we have for Lynn, Lisa and Brandy let's analyze their emotions. Managing your emotions is the second key for powerful communication. This process will work for the person sending the message and the person receiving the message. For Lynn anyone violating her daughters' safety is a trigger toward anger. Taking off work is another trigger.

Let's use the red, yellow, and green colors of a traffic light to determine how to act. Like a traffic light, red represents danger if you proceed. Look at the next page at how the color red points in four different directions.

When emotions are red (anger, fear, shame, etc.), the conversation can go in any direction. This may be an explosive situation. Yellow represents caution. Notice there are two arrows. You can go up to red or you can go down to green. If your emotions are calm, then let green represent those emotions. Green then is the time to act. If your emotions are red or yellow you may want to handle getting them to green before communicating. Like with the traffic light, timing can impact your message.

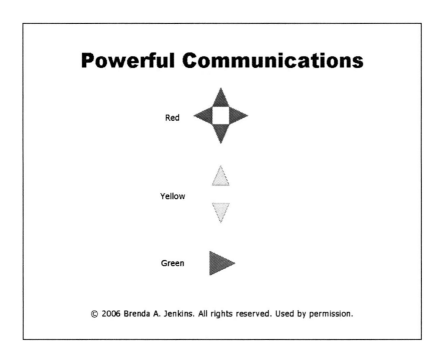

What if Lynn went up to the school the same day the fight took place and demanded answers? Let's add color to our emotions on the Emotions Chart #2.

Emotions – Chart #2

Knowledge	Emotions	Does this have anything to do with what you want to communicate at this time?	Act with Purpose
Lynn – lost time (money) having to leave work early.	Red		
Lynn – Her daughters are not safe – fight at school.	Red		
Lynn – She has spoken to Brandy's teacher twice in the last 3 months.	Red		
Lisa – jumped into the fight to protect her sister.	Red		
Lisa – acts as if this is just another day at school.	Green		
Brandy – is crying.	Red		
Brandy – is worried about the impact this incident will have on her status in honor society.	Red		
Brandy – wants to change schools.	Red		
Brandy – feels she had to defend herself and it is not fair she is being excluded.	Red		

The chart shows Lisa's emotions are red and green while both Lynn and Brandy's emotions are all red. Using our definition of red this is not the time to be dealing with the issue by trying to communicate with others. This is a time for getting our reds down to green. Lynn may want to start with herself since she is the parent. Start by focusing on the immediate concern. What is her immediate concern? Let's say it is helping Brandy settle down. Now by looking at just Lynn's data, let's see what information has to do with the immediate goal of getting Brandy settled. See Chart # 3.

Lynn's Data – Chart # 3

Knowledge	Emotions	GOAL: Settle Brandy down	Act with Purpose
Lynn – lost time (money) having to leave work early.	Red	This is not part of helping Brandy.	
Lynn – Her daughters are not safe – fight at school.	Red	This is not part of helping Brandy.	
Lynn – She has spoken to Brandy's teacher twice in the last 3 months.	Red	This is not part of helping Brandy.	

Please note the importance of timing. Now is not the time to deal with any of Lynn's emotions. While Lynn's concerns are valid, right now it is not about Lynn. The goal is settling Brandy down and getting Lisa to express her emotions. Powerful communication means that the message has a goal and when emotions are calm enough (green) to *act with purpose*; it is all about the person you want to receive the message. Lynn's goal is to settle Brandy down.

ACT WITH PURPOSE

After you acquire knowledge and manage your emotions, concentrate on your goal. This may assist you as you decide upon the actions you will use to communicate your message. Lynn has to consider all she knows about Brandy's emotions and concerns. What does she know? Lynn knows Brandy is upset, concerned about her status in the honor society, feels she had no choice but to defend herself and she wants to change schools. Lynn also knows that Brandy never wanted to go to this school. She applied to other high schools but because of other issues Lynn decided to send Brandy to the neighborhood school with Lisa.

Following are some suggested actions Lynn may use to help Brandy settle down. She can provide safety, warmth and an ear to hear her fears. Lynn can tell Brandy that together they will review the requirements of the honor society and work out what needs to be done to keep her in the society. Lynn assures Brandy that if she is put on probation that is not the end of the world. It means she has a second chance. Lynn can tell Brandy that they will revisit the issue of changing schools. She will look at possibilities with the goal of changing schools at semester break. Again timing is important. Lynn does not want to move Brandy in the middle of a semester. She will explain to Brandy how such a move may impact her grades and impact her membership in the honors society because of possible fallen grades. Lynn can explain to Brandy the school policy, explaining the consequences of breaking policy and more importantly have Brandy take responsibility for her actions. Explain that when you take responsibility for your actions then you can do something about them. Look at Brandy's emotions in Chart #4.

Brandy's Emotions – Chart #4

Knowledge	Emotions	GOAL: Settle Brandy down	Lynn's Actions with Purpose
Brandy – is crying.	Red	Safety Warmth	Hold her daughter in her arms. Kiss her and let her tell you all her fears.
Brandy – is worried about impact this incident will have on her status in honor society.	Red	Responsibility Accountability	Lynn will review with Brandy the policy for membership in the honor society. They will work within the guidelines.
Brandy – wants to change schools.	Red	Impact of timing Analytical skills	Lynn tells Brandy that she is going to look into other schools with the target date of change being at the close of the current semester.
Brandy – feels she had to defend herself and it is not fair she is being excluded.	Red	Responsibility Accountability	Lynn tells Brandy that she has to take responsibility for her actions. She tells Brandy to think of ways the fight may have been prevented.

Now let's look at Lisa. She had one red. Her green is also a concern for Lynn because of her knowledge of Lisa. Lynn realizes that Lisa has adapted to the violence at the school. Lisa's grades are bad and she does not show emotions. Lynn knows that being in touch with your emotions helps with life issues. Lynn shares with Lisa that her strength comes from within but that she also knows she needs to be able to express her feelings in a safe place. Lynn is holding her daughter and ensures her she is in a safe place now. Look at Lisa's Chart # 5.

Lisa's Emotions – Chart # 5

Knowledge	Emotions	GOAL: Helping Lisa share her feelings	Lynn's Actions with Purpose
Lisa – jumped in fight to protect her sister.	Red	Responsibility Accountability	Hold her daughter in her arms. Kiss her and ask her "what questions" to try to get her in touch with her feelings.
Lisa – acts as if this is just another day at school.	Green	Dealing with emotions in safe place.	No action.

As a lighthouse, Lynn has shown her daughters the following skills: problem-solving, taking responsibility, being accountable for her actions, being flexible (ability to change her mind about the decision to send Brandy to another school), dealing with emotions in a safe place and the importance of timing. By managing her emotions and showing concern for her daughters Lynn demonstrated putting her daughter's needs before her needs. Lynn deals with her needs at another time (near the end of the chapter).

The concern that Lynn had was the safety of her teens in the unsupervised areas of the school (lunchroom, bathroom and common areas). Using the same three principles of acquiring knowledge, managing emotions and acting with purpose, Lynn can be a powerful communicator with the school staff.

At her meeting with the school staff two weeks later, Lynn and her daughters accepted responsibility and the consequences of their actions. The girls were admitted back to school. Lynn made a separate appointment requesting a support team to meet with her to discuss the safety of her daughters in the unsupervised areas of the school. She stated this was a concern and wanted input from the staff on how they could work together. Since safety at school is a responsibility of the school, Lynn is working in partnership with the staff. The staff was delighted to meet with Lynn. She also started attending the parent support group.

Lynn worked through her daughters' issues. But she also had her own issues to deal with. Her emotions are now green. Now it was time to look at hers. Using the same principles, let's look at Chart #6 to see her actions for herself.

Lynn's Actions – Chart # 6

Knowledge	Emotions	Goal	Act with Purpose
Lynn – lost time (money) having to leave work early.	Green	Take responsibility for the job she currently has.	1. Talk with her boss about working flex time and show the benefits this would bring to the company. 2. Look for job that pays more money and one that she would like to do. 3. Determine the skills needed. 4. List skills she currently has and those she will need. 5. Work on developing the skills needed for the job. 6. Set a time frame for having the skills needed.
Lynn – Her daughters are not safe – fight at school.	Green	Hold the High School accountable. Join the parent group.	Going to the next level to get the needed results.
Lynn – She has spoken to Brandy's teacher twice in the last 3 months.	Green	Same as above.	Same as above.

As our children see how we act, they in turn will act. Our goal is making sure our children are not left behind. That's why we need to make decisions that get the most from our communications in the least amount of time.

This is about effectively using the time we have to train our children. Time is a valuable commodity.

To understand your child's challenges, you will need to see the challenge from their point of view. This will require good communication skills on your part. On Chart #7 you see possible outcome from Lynn's actions when her emotions are red. Do you think those types of actions move Lynn closer to the goal of assuring that her daughters are not left behind?

Lynn's Possible Actions with "RED" Emotions – Chart #7

Knowledge	Emotions	GOAL	Act with purpose
Lynn – lost time (money) having to leave work early.	Red	1. Blaming	1. Calls child's father stating it is his fault why she is working. States she can not handle taking off work to go to the school
		2. Defending	2. Tells boss she had to leave because her child needs her. Explains she is a single parent.
		3. Not understanding other's perception	3. Did not consider what impact her leaving her job would have on the company.
		4. Not staying focused on the goal.	4. If the goal is the lost money actions have not dealt with that.
		5. Not knowing impact of time.	5. Just left job.
		6. Not caring about others.	6. Just left job.

Lynn's Possible Actions with "RED" Emotions – Chart #7

Lynn – Her daughters are not safe – fight at school.	Red	1. Blaming	1. Stating the school is not doing their responsibility.
		2. Defending	2. The school is always having fights. "I hate that school."
		3. Not understanding other's perception	3. Stating the staff at school is not doing anything.
		4. Not staying focused on the healthy goal.	
Lynn – She has spoken to Brandy's teacher twice in the last 3 months.	Red	1. Blaming	1. Furious about having talked with teacher twice with no results. States teacher does not care and did not do anything.
		2. Defending	2. I have done my part. I went up to the school twice.
		3. Not understanding other's perception	3. States teacher does not care and did not do anything.

Once you understand others, you increase the likelihood that they will try to understand you. Knowledge, management of emotions and actions that are purposefully delivered are the keys to enable anyone to become powerful and influential as a communicator. Powerful communication can be accomplished with two powerful communicators or with one powerful communicator that cares.

As with Lynn these are also skills to help you develop yourself. I challenge you to become a powerful communicator in all areas of your life. This is a continuous lifelong process.

POWERFUL COMMUNICATIONS

- **First – Be a learner.** Get as much information about the topic and person/people (audience and yourself).

- **Second – Manage your emotions** and your reactions to others.

- **Third – Act with Purpose** (If you are the messenger, it is <u>not</u> about you. If you are the receiver, it is about you, so ask questions and validate the message).

Goal (Stay Focused)

Powerful Communications

Red **First - Be a learner.**
Get as much information about the topic, persons and yourself. DO NOT ACT!

Yellow **Second – Manage your emotions**
and your reactions to others. DO NOT ACT!

Green **Third – ACT WITH PURPOSE!**
(If you are the messenger, it is <u>not</u> about you. If you are the receiver, it is about you so ask questions).

© 2006 Brenda A. Jenkins. All rights reserved. Used by permission.

EXERCISES

1. List ways you communicate to your child that you care. Have your child list things that they think you do that show you care. Compare the two lists. If their list does not match your list, make sure you understand everything on their list. Then work on ways using the three principles to help them understand that you do care. Remember, they may not be able to connect that you working all the time shows that you love them. You may need to show the benefits that are directly related to them from your working.

2. Pick someone that does not listen to you and listen to them quietly. Listen without your perception.
Write down their perception of the topic being discussed.

Now from their perception try to communicate your point using the three principles explained in this chapter. Were your results different? Were you able to powerfully communicate?

3. At your next meeting, (Bible study, Parent Teacher Association, etc.) listen to hear the point and then ask questions to make sure you understand their point. Ask the speaker for validation of your understanding.

4. List and examine how others perceive you. You may want to start with those you care about and then work on the rest. Don't defend yourself. Now examine your list. Ask yourself do they know you? Do you want them to know you? Work to resolve the differences.

5. Write down your actions that trigger red emotions in you. For each red emotion write what happened before you felt the emotion. Can you change what happen? If not, write down your possible actions that help you execute your goal. ACT with purpose!

6. When someone close to you has an emotion that is red, write down how that makes you feel. Think of how to act with purpose in order to help the other person. Remember what the message is that you want to deliver. Think about how Lynn handled her emotions from the example in this chapter.

7. If you tried the first six exercises, write down your evaluation on how powerful a communicator you are.

If your evaluation is that your communication is still weak, redo the first six exercises. Try using different people.

SUGGESTIONS:
1. Listen to understand the perception of others first. Do not add too or finish their message.
2. Inquire for understanding. Know the perception of the other person(s). Put their perception in your own words. Have the person receiving the message validate what you said in their own words.
3. Guide other people by starting at their perception to get to your perception.
4. Healthy parents nourish ongoing effective communications.
5. Time is an important resource. Reduce the communication wasters:
    - Blaming
    - Defending
    - Not understanding other's perception
    - Not staying focused on the topic or goal
    - Not knowing the impact of time
    - Not caring about others

If you put these exercises to daily use, you will not only be a powerful communicator, you will demonstrate the kind of communication skills that will show your children how to communicate with power as well. And being able to communicate well is a major step toward not being left behind.

Show me now

How do I know you care?

I hear all your problems,

Do you hear mine?

I see your pain,

Do you see mine?

How do I handle my problems?

I watch how you handle yours.

How do I handle my pain?

I watch how you handle yours.

See I am just like you.

I am showing you I care.

I love you.

B. Springer

Conclusion

"Liberty lies in the hearts of men and women; when it dies there, no constitution, no law, no court can save it."
- Judge Learned Hand

In the introduction we discussed the village concept (the posse). We hope that after reading these pages you are motivated to use the skills that you have to share, first with your child and then with others in the community.

The foundation of the pyramid has been laid. We now understand that keeping ourselves healthy (physically, mentally, emotionally and spiritually) is vital for us to reach our goals. We trust that you are committed to staying focused on the goal of raising healthy offspring by acquiring knowledge, managing your emotions and acting with purpose, which is an important key to powerful communications.

If we did not have advanced technology, money or earthly valuables what do we have left? Is it integrity, respect and love? These may be the most important concepts we can teach our youth. Think of time as a valuable commodity like money. Once the time and money are gone, we cannot get them back. When we have the money we can invest it wisely for a greater return. With children, we need to invest our time with them. We may get an even greater return. With all your heart stay focused on your goal.

Recap

Make every moment a teaching moment.
It may save some time and money.

Be honest with yourself.

Take care of yourself and your family.

If you find yourself slipping into old patterns remember to ask yourself, "What do you know for sure?"

When communicating with others, use the three principles you've learned so your communications can be powerful!

Recommended Reading

1. Abena Safiyah Fousa, Mother Wit-365 Meditations for African-American Women, 1996, Abingdon Press, Nashville, TN.37202

2. Dr. James Dobson, Complete Marriage and Family Home Reference Guide, 2000 – Tyndale House Publishers, Inc. Wheaton, IL

3. Carl R. Boyd, Plain Teaching-49 Lessons on Being a Positive Teacher-1991-Advice Media Publications c/o Ruth Jones – 2235 East 70th Street, Kansas City, MO. 64132

4. Carl R. Boyd, Last of the Old School Educators. (2001). Advice Media Publications c/o Ruth Jones – 2235 East 70th Street, Kansas City, MO. 64132

5. Hayes-Scott, Fairy C.PhD, ed. Martin, Nora Ph.D. Consultant, Parents Imparting Discipline & Heritage. (1998). Robbie Dean Press, Ann Arbor, MI.

6. Dr. Jawanza Kunjufu. Restoring the Village. (1996) African American Images, Chicago, Illinois.

7. David Niven, PH.D. The 100 Simple Secrets of Healthy People -2003-Harper San Francisco, A Division of Harper Collins Publisher

8. Dr. Virginia F. Lewis, Short Stories From a Long Career, 2005- Third World Press, Chicago, Illinois.

9. Dr. Phil McGraw, Family First, 2004-Simon and Schuster, Inc. Audio Division, 1230 Avenue of the Americas, New York, NY. 10020

About Brenda A. Jenkins

Brenda loves people. She states her purpose is to take her gifts and skills to help others. She is very transparent and has no problem sharing her victories overcoming rough times in her life. Brenda has the ability to see the expected outcome of any task and works to put plans in place to reach that end.

Brenda is well-versed in problem-solving, organizational and interpersonal skills. The foundation for all that she does is anchored in her strong commitment to the Word of God. She is the mother to four adult children and the proud grandmother to twelve grandchildren.

At New Hope Missionary Baptist Church in Southfield, Michigan, Brenda served faithfully for seven years as the Ministry Director of the Biblical Counseling Ministry; a ministry birthed under her leadership. She has also served as the Counseling Advisor and Outreach Facilitator for this ministry. As a Certified Biblical Counselor and adjunct instructor for Christian Research and Development, she teaches classes that will build up students and prepare them to confront themselves and counsel others with the Bible as the guidebook.

As CEO of ARIEL Connections her passion is "Providing Relationship Solutions to Organizations that Value People."

For more information or to book Ms. Jenkins for speaking engagements, or radio and television interviews contact:

ARIEL Connections
P. O. Box 22 ▪ Royal Oak, MI 48068-0022
Email: brenda.jenkins@ariel-connections.com
Website: www.ARIEL-Connections.com
Toll Free: (866) 280-3378
Phone: (248) 355-3949

A - Accept
R - Relate
I - Invest
E - Encourage
L - Love

About Dr. Loretta J. Martin

Dr. Loretta J. Martin is a retired Chicago Public School teacher, counselor and administrator who successfully ran the largest Driver Education Program in the nation. She has also taught part time at Northeastern Illinois University and Northwestern University. She has taught parenting classes and has been a state certified addictions counselor for the past ten years.

She is one of the last of the "old school" educators who is still in touch with hundreds of her former students. A curious colleague once asked a student, "Why do you all love Martin so much?" The reply was, "Because she is such a good role model." To Loretta, that is one of the greatest compliments that anyone who works with children, could receive.

In addition to her national speaking engagements in schools, conferences, churches and retreats, she has traveled to five countries in Africa, as well as to Europe, South America and various islands in Central America. In her travels she visits schools and homes in order to assess the differences and commonalities of educational practices and the culture of the people.

Loretta is an active member of Trinity United Church of Christ, Delta Sigma Theta Sorority, Inc. and three alumni groups at Wendell Phillips High School Academy. She also volunteers as a mentor and provides tutorial services for the students. In her spare time, she teaches line dancing and Chicago Style Stepping to adults and children.

She is the Founder and President of the Hall-Martin Foundation, Inc. that has awarded scholarships to graduating high school seniors for the past 23 years. Loretta and her four adult children are investors in real estate and operate a family owned Smoothie Factory business in Dallas, Texas. This closely knit family prays together every Sunday night with a conference call. Their love for each other is expressed openly and they are leaving a legacy for their children and for generations to come.

Loretta and her smooth dancing partner can be seen weekly on the TV show "Can I Step with You" on Channel 19 in Chicago and they recently performed at the world famous Chicago Theater in a musical titled, "Serendipity - Seniors on Stage." Seated proudly in the audience were her children, grandchildren and great grandchildren. "Now that's what I call "flipping the script" says Loretta. "Grandmas are usually in the audience."

For more information or to book Dr. Martin for speaking engagements, or radio and television interviews contact:

Hall-Martin Legacy Foundation, Inc.
P.O. Box 49612 ▪ Chicago, IL. 60649
Phone (773) 520-6072 ▪ Fax (773) 768-3471
Website: Hall-MartinLegacyFoundationInc.com
E-mail: Retta425@aol.com

When We Reach the Edge, Where Do We Go for Support?

Name _____

Address _____

City _____ State _____ Zip _____

Phone _____ Fax _____

Email _____

Quantity	
Price *(each)*	$4.99
Subtotal	
S & H *(each)*	$0.99
MI Tax 6%	
TOTAL	

METHOD OF PAYMENT:
☐ Check or Money Order
(*Make payable to*: **PriorityONE Publications**)
☐ Visa   ☐ Master Card   ☐ American Express
Acct No. _____
Expiration Date (*mmyy*) _____
Signature _____

Mail your payment with this form to:
PriorityONE Publications
P. O. Box 725, Farmington, MI 48332
(800) 331-8841 – Toll Free
(313) 893-3359 – Southeast Michigan
URL: http://www.p1pubs.com
Email: info@p1pubs.com

Leaving the Lone Ranger Mentality – Alone!

Name _____

Address _____

City _____ State _____ Zip _____

Phone _____ Fax _____

Email _____

Quantity	
Price *(each)*	$4.99
Subtotal	
S & H *(each)*	$0.99
MI Tax 6%	
TOTAL	

METHOD OF PAYMENT:
☐ Check or Money Order
(*Make payable to*: **PriorityONE Publications**)
☐ Visa   ☐ Master Card   ☐ American Express
Acct No. _____
Expiration Date (*mmyy*) _____
Signature _____

Mail your payment with this form to:
PriorityONE Publications
P. O. Box 725, Farmington, MI 48332
(800) 331-8841 – Toll Free
(313) 893-3359 – Southeast Michigan
URL: http://www.p1pubs.com
Email: info@p1pubs.com

HELP! for Your Leadership

Name _____

Address _____

City _____ State _____ Zip _____

Phone _____ Fax _____

Email _____

Quantity	
Price *(each)*	$14.99
Subtotal	
S & H *(each)*	$2.99
MI Tax 6%	
TOTAL	

METHOD OF PAYMENT:
☐ Check or Money Order
(*Make payable to*: **PriorityONE Publications**)
☐ Visa   ☐ Master Card   ☐ American Express
Acct No. _____
Expiration Date (*mmyy*) _____
Signature _____

Mail your payment with this form to:
PriorityONE Publications
P. O. Box 725, Farmington, MI 48332
(800) 331-8841 – Toll Free
(313) 893-3359 – Southeast Michigan
URL: http://www.p1pubs.com
Email: info@p1pubs.com

HELP! for Your Leadership Workbook

Name _____

Address _____

City _____ State _____ Zip _____

Phone _____ Fax _____

Email _____

Quantity		
Price *(each)*		$10.99
Subtotal		
S & H *(each)*		$2.99
MI Tax 6%		
TOTAL		

METHOD OF PAYMENT:
☐ Check or Money Order
(*Make payable to*: **PriorityONE Publications**)
☐ Visa   ☐ Master Card   ☐ American Express
Acct No. _____
Expiration Date (*mmyy*) _____
Signature _____

Mail your payment with this form to:
PriorityONE Publications
P. O. Box 725, Farmington, MI 48332
(800) 331-8841 – Toll Free
(313) 893-3359 – Southeast Michigan
URL: http://www.p1pubs.com
Email: info@p1pubs.com

He is NOT Left Behind... He is with ME!

Name _____

Address _____

City _____ State _____ Zip _____

Phone _____ Fax _____

Email _____

Quantity	
Price *(each)*	$9.99
Subtotal	
S & H *(each)*	$1.99
MI Tax 6%	
TOTAL	

METHOD OF PAYMENT:
☐ Check or Money Order
(*Make payable to*: **PriorityONE Publications**)
☐ Visa   ☐ Master Card   ☐ American Express
Acct No. _____
Expiration Date (*mmyy*) _____
Signature _____

Mail your payment with this form to:
PriorityONE Publications
P. O. Box 725, Farmington, MI 48332
(800) 331-8841 – Toll Free
(313) 893-3359 – Southeast Michigan
URL: http://www.p1pubs.com
Email: info@p1pubs.com

Printed in the United States
87879LV00003B/160-429/A